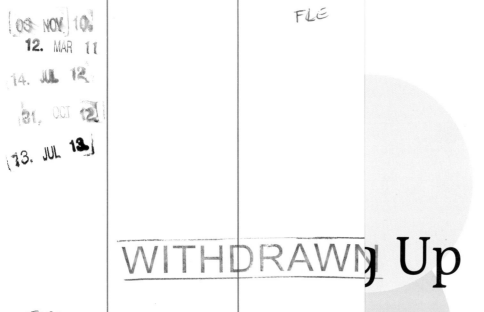

Up

nnabel Spenceley

l Underwood

Hampshire
County Council

A CHERRYTREE BOOK

This edition first published in 2007
by Cherrytree Books, part of
The Evans Publishing Group Limited
2a Portman Mansions
Chiltern Street
London W1U 6NR

Printed in China

Amos, Janine
    Owning up. - Rev. ed. - (Growing up)
    1. Truthfulness and falsehood - Pictorial works - Juvenile
    literature 2. Conscience - Pictorial works - Juvenile
    literature
    I. Title
    177.3

ISBN 9781842344965

CREDITS
Editor: Louise John
Designer: D.R.ink
Photography: Gareth Boden
Production: Jenny Mulvanny

Based on the original edition of Owning Up published in 1997

With thanks to: Nicholas and Alice Turpin, Edward Evans and Nahal Rao

Alice and Dad

The kitchen's
a mess.

Dad cleans
it up.

5

He washes the dishes.
He cleans the floor.

He clears the table.
He throws all the
rubbish away.

Alice comes in. "Where's my model?" she asks. "It was on the table."

Dad looks at Alice.
He looks at the bin.

"I made a mistake, Alice,"
says Dad. "I put your model
in the bin."

Alice is upset.
Her dad gives
her a hug.

"I'm sorry," says Dad.
"That model was important
to you, wasn't it?"

Alice nods her head.
How does she feel?

"Why don't we find somewhere safe to keep your models?" says Dad. "How about that cupboard?"

"Yes!" agrees Alice.
"We'll need to empty
it first," Dad tells her.

"Let's do it now!" says Alice.
"OK," says Dad.

Alice makes another model.

And then Dad clears up the kitchen again!

Building Models

"Chug! Chug! I'm building a tractor," says Edward.

Edward works hard. The tractor is finished. He looks in the box for a driver.

Nahal comes to build a train.

He picks up Edward's tractor and pulls it apart. He uses the tractor to make his train.

"Hey! Where's my tractor?"
Edward asks.
"I used it in my train," says Nahal.
"I didn't know."

How do you think
Edward feels?
How does Nahal feel?
What could they do?

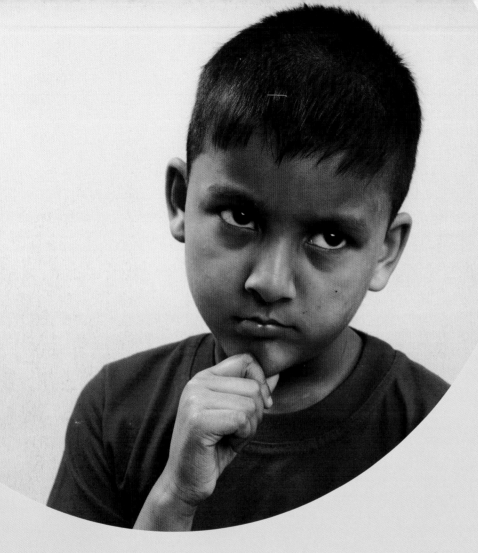

Nahal thinks hard.
"You can play with
my train," he says.

"But I want a tractor," Edward tells him.

"What shall we do?" asks Nahal.

"We could make this into a new tractor," says Edward.

"Yes – with great big wheels!" agrees Nahal.

Together they build a
new tractor.

Teachers' Notes

The following extension activities will assist teachers in delivering aspects of the PSHE and Citizenship Framework as well as aspects of the Healthy Schools criteria.

Specific areas supported are:

- Framework for PSHE&C 1b, 1c, 1e, 2a, 2e, 2h, 4a, 4b, 4d, 5b, 5f
- National Healthy School Criteria 1.1, 4.3

Activity for *Alice and Dad*

Read the story to the children.

- Show the children the picture of Dad when he realises what he has done – ask the children how they think he feels at that moment. It is an 'Oh no!' moment.
- Ask the children if they have ever felt like that.
- Tell them that everyone makes mistakes. Share an example of a time when you made a mistake.
- Invite the children to share a time when they made a mistake or had an 'Oh no!' moment.
- Explain that when we realise we have made a mistake and we own up we can then try to make things better again.
- Ask the children who shared their own experiences how they made things better again.
- Draw a 'choice chart' for Dad on the board. Write 'Dad' in the centre of the board and then put his choices up like a spider diagram. Ask the children what those choices might be, e.g.
    He could have said it was Alice's fault for leaving her model on the table.
    He could have said the cat knocked it on the floor and broke it.
    He could have got angry with Alice for the mess.
- Remind the children that everyone makes mistakes and that when you feel that 'Oh no!' feeling you have choices. Only one choice lets you make things right again and that is owning up to what you have done.

Activity for *Building Models*

Read the story to the children.

- Then, with the children in a circle, talk them through the story up to the point where Edward asks, 'Where's my tractor?'
- This time ask the children to think of a different answer that Nahal might give.
- Why might he give a different answer?
- Ask for two children to volunteer to 'act out' the story using the new ideas with Nahal not taking responsibility for his actions.
- Ask the children to notice how this new ending is different.
- How does Edward feel now?
- How does Nahal feel now?
- Re-enact the story as it is in the book.
- Ask the children to identify how the characters feel at the end of the book.
- Which ending do the children think was best?